Life at Sea

Margaret Rule

Wayland

Titles in the series

Clothes   Kings and Queens

Country Life   Life at Sea

Exploration   Religion

Food   Scientists and Writers

Homes   Town Life

Cover illustrations: *Background* One of the earliest charts, 1539;
inset The Spanish Armada, painted in the late sixteenth century.

First published in 1994 by Wayland (Publishers) Ltd
61 Western Road, Hove, East Sussex, BN3 1JD, England

Editor: Cath Senker
Designer: John Christopher
Picture researcher: Elizabeth Moore

British Library Cataloguing in Publication Data
Margaret Rule
Life at Sea. – (Tudors and Stuarts series)
I. Title II. Series
387.50941

ISBN 0-7502-1110-5

Typeset by Strong Silent Type
Printed and bound by B.P.C.C. Paulton Books, Great Britain

Notes for teachers

Life at Sea draws on a wide range of exciting sources, including maps, artefacts, models and paintings. This book:

◆ looks at the tools and equipment which made it possible for Tudor and Stuart sailors to make long voyages;

◆ describes how battles were fought at sea, and which weapons were used;

◆ explains the rules followed on board ship;

◆ helps the reader to understand what life was like for ordinary sailors – what they ate, the work they did and how they entertained themselves;

◆ describes the roles of different people, such as the Barber-Surgeon and the Carpenter;

◆ gives diagrams showing how to tie some of the knots used in sailing;

◆ shows the reader how we can use direct evidence from shipwrecks and clues from ship models, paintings and writing to learn about life at sea in Tudor and Stuart times.

Picture acknowledgements
Archaeological Diving Unit 23; Ashmolean Museum, Oxford 11;
Bridgeman *cover* (inset), *title page*, 26 (National Maritime Museum); City of Portsmouth 15 (below), Magdalene College, Cambridge 24; Mary Rose Trust *cover* (background), 4, 5, 6, 7 (above), 8 (C Dobbs), 9 (below), 12 (both), 13, 14, 15 (above), 16 (both), 17, 18, 21, 25 (above); National Maritime Museum, London 19 (above), 22; Rex Features 7 (below), 27 (below); The Board of the Trustees of the Royal Armouries (Object VII-1267) 9 (above); Science Museum 25 (below); R Sheridan Art and Architecture Collection 27 (above); Vasa Museum, Sweden 10 (both). Artwork on pages 6, 19, 20, 21 and 26 by Steve Wheele.

Contents

The dangers of the sea

Life at sea has always been dangerous. Even today, ships are sometimes lost at sea in storms and small fishing boats can disappear without trace. During the time of the Tudors and Stuarts (1485 to 1714) life at sea was very dangerous indeed.

In early Tudor times good navigation tools were invented, so a navigator could work out the position of his ship on the ocean and plot a course on his charts (sea maps).

A navigator in the sixteenth century could plan his route across the sea and, most importantly, find his way home again.

Tudor navigation tools.

1 Slide protractor

2 Plotting board

3 Pocket sundial

4 Lid of sundial

5 Dividers

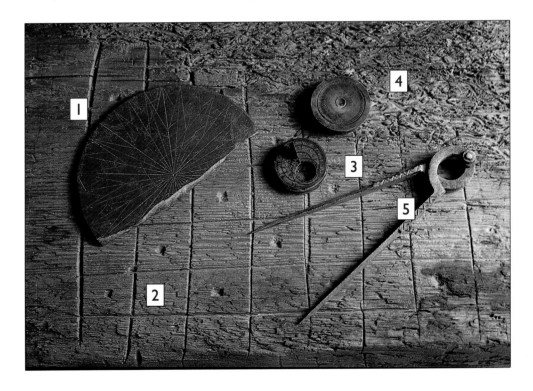

This sixteenth-century chart shows the rich fishing grounds north of the mainland of Scotland. The map-maker shows some of the dangers a seaman would face if he sailed from the Orkneys, a group of islands in the south-west, up to the large island of Greenland in the north-west.

This chart from 1539 shows Greenland, Iceland, Shetland and the Orkneys (called Orcades). You can see sea monsters in the water.

You can see large ships being attacked by monster fish. Seamen imagined these creatures, but the monsters were probably based on tales of large whales, which spouted water and could overturn small boats.

Find a modern chart of northern Britain, Iceland and Greenland. Compare it with the chart made in 1539. Modern charts are usually very accurate. But in 1992 a large passenger ship, the *Queen Elizabeth II*, ran aground near the coast of the USA with hundreds of holiday-makers on board. This was partly because of bad charts which showed the wrong depth of water. No one was hurt, but the ship was damaged a little.

A Tudor gun drill

Seafaring merchants defended their right to fish and to carry trade goods to and from the continent of Europe. Most ships carried guns even in peacetime.

In wartime, merchant ships were seized by the king or queen and armed with more guns and trained soldiers. Then, when the war was over, the ship was again used to carry passengers and goods.

(Below) A model of the gun decks on Henry VIII's warship, the _Mary Rose_.

Firing a cast bronze muzzle-loading gun

2. This man places shot in the barrel and rams it to the back. He puts in a piece of wood called a wad as well.

1. This man loads gunpowder in through the muzzle.

Touch hole with a little gunpowder on it.

Barrel

Muzzle

Pile of shot

4. Gunpowder in the barrel explodes and forces shot out of the gun.

3. Master gunner lights the gunpowder in the touch hole using a linstock with a match in it.

Below left is a full-scale model of part of the two gun decks on the Tudor warship, the *Mary Rose*. The gunner is about to fire an iron breech-loading gun from the lower deck. Next to the iron breech-loading gun is a cast bronze gun. Behind the gunner there is a ladder leading to the upper deck. An archer fires from the upper deck.

(Right) Some of the kinds of shot used in early guns, including solid shot of stone and iron, lead shot, and lead which was cast or wrapped around a central pellet of iron.

1 Stone shot.

2 Different kinds of lead shot.

3 Stone mould used for casting shot.

(Left) HMS Hermes returning to Britain after the Battle of the Falklands in the South Atlantic, 1982.

This modern ship could fire very accurate missiles. A Tudor or Stuart Admiral would have been amazed by its weapons!

War at sea

A Tudor warship was a floating platform for guns. The gunners aimed to damage the enemy ship and slow her down in the early stages of a battle. It was the job of the Captain to bring the ship into the correct position so that his big guns could damage or disable the enemy ship. The ship's Master gave all the commands to the sailors to steer the ship. The Master Gunner told the gunners when to load and fire.

The second stage of a battle was fought at closer range. Archers on the *Mary Rose* could shoot their pointed iron-tipped arrows 200 metres. The arrows could pierce the body armour worn by the officers on the enemy ships.

From the 1550s onwards musketeers using handguns took over from archers.

Here is the author underwater looking at a box of longbows from the *Mary Rose*, which sank in 1545. The wreck was excavated in the 1980s.

A late sixteenth-century bill made of steel. Mounted on a long pole, it could be used to slash and stab the enemy.

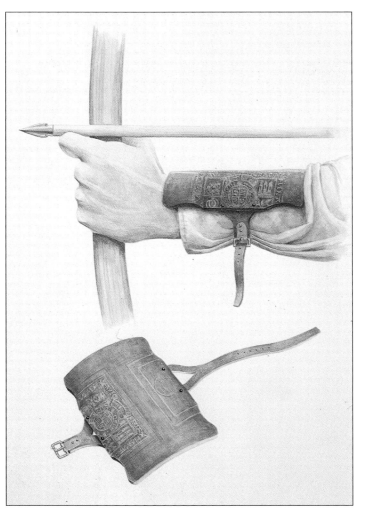

In Tudor and Stuart times, weapons such as guns, swords, pikes and bills were all used when the enemy came closer. Stores of hand weapons were kept 'ready to use' close to the masts on the upper decks.

In the sixteenth century the Captain of a ship would try to disable an enemy ship and then go on board and capture her. Ships were too valuable to sink, and captured guns were much too useful to send to the bottom of the sea.

Drawing a longbow. The archer wears a leather wrist-guard. The arrow is tipped with a dart-like arrowhead which could pierce armour.

Who was in command?

The safety of a ship depends on everyone knowing who is in command. In 1530 Henry VIII introduced orders which every member of the crew had to obey. There were punishments for not obeying the Captain or other officers. Stealing from other sailors and falling asleep on duty were major crimes.

(Below) A modern photo of the Admiral's cabin on the early seventeenth-century Swedish ship, *Wasa*. It is richly decorated and furnished. The cabin boy is helping the admiral to dress.

(Above) This model is wearing clothes made from cloth and leather found on the *Wasa*. Sailors wore clothes like these.

The Lord High Admiral, Lord Clinton, painted in 1562 holding a steering compass.

Timeline

1492
The first globe is made in Nuremberg (in what is now Germany) by Martin Behaim.

1509
Work begins on building the *Mary Rose* in Portsmouth.

1530
Henry VIII introduces orders to be obeyed on ship.

1545
The *Mary Rose* sinks.

1550
Musketeers using handguns begin to take over from archers in sea battles.

Officers were responsible to their Captain, and the captains in the fleet were responsible to the Admiral. Battle tactics were discussed by the captains and the Admiral before battle began.

The ships could not be sailed against the wind. If any ship lost the advantage of the wind it took a long time to bring it back into the battle fleet. Often a Captain had to chase and attack the enemy without support from other ships.

Many years later, in 1653, the Commonwealth Navy had a battle plan involving large numbers of ships. This was possible because it had become much easier to move ships around.

The life of a sailor

In towns with ports, such as Bristol, Leith, London and Plymouth, many young men went to sea. They learned to be sailors on merchant ships, but served the king or queen in wartime.

For most of 1590, John Baker, aged fifteen, served as a younker (youngster) on the *Hopewell*, an armed merchant ship. John Baker is an imaginary boy, but he is just like many who learned their trade on merchant ships. His father was a landowner and John learned reading, writing and arithmetic at a grammar school before he went to sea at the age of fourteen.

A backgammon board from the *Mary Rose*. Dice and board games were always popular among seamen.

The *Hopewell* set sail from Plymouth on 20 March with two other ships, to carry out pirate attacks on Spanish ships carrying trade goods to and from the West Indies. She returned to Plymouth on 24 October.

A small bosun's call, a whistle which was used to signal orders to the seamen. It hung around the neck on a silk cord, like a referee's whistle.

Here is a part of John Baker's diary:

Monday 21 September 1590 at six o'clock in the evening

As today I had no other duties the Boatswain [Bosun] asked the Quartermaster to issue the boys with fishing tackle and in these rich waters we soon had a good catch.

My friend Simon is the Barber-Surgeon's Mate and he has been very busy. There are many on board with sores which will not heal and he has been preparing healing ointments using herbs and good fat prepared from beef suet. We have taken on sweet water and we caught enough fish to have fresh food today. The Barber-Surgeon says this will help the men who are sick.

The Carpenter has been busy checking the leathers on the pumps. We have three pumps, one by the main mast, one forward towards the bow and one aft of amidships [towards the middle of the boat]. If the leathers wear, the pump does not suck well and no one likes to work the pump handle for no return. It is hard work but with many working together, we can keep the ship dry.

Musical instruments: tabor pipes, a drumstick and part of a Tudor fiddle.

I took my dinner and ate it in a quiet corner on the deck because the weather is fine and it was good to get away from the hold where I normally eat and sleep. After dinner I heard the Trumpeter, whose job is to sound commands, play the tabor pipe for the Captain, Master White and the Master in the stern cabin. He is a good musician. They say that, on the Queen's great ships, this often happens but it is rare on the Hopewell *and it may mean that we are soon bound for home.*

Food and drink

The *Mary Rose* sank in 1545. When the wreck was excavated in the 1980s archaeologists found meat and fish bones in casks (barrels). They could see from the bones that joints of meat had been carefully chosen. Parts of the animal which were rich in fat and would go bad quickly were not included. The meat was chopped from animals of the same age and size and cut into standard lumps.

Beef bones from a cask of salt beef found on the *Mary Rose*.

In 1565, certain food standards on board ship became law. The amount of food allowed for each man was just enough to keep him fit. A man was allowed the following rations each week:

7 lbs (3 kg) of biscuits
7 gallons (26.5 litres) of beer
8 lbs (3.6 kg) of salt beef
3/4 lb (340 g) of stock fish
3/8 lb (170 g) of butter
3/4 lb (340 g) of cheese

These rations were cooked all together. Usually the food was boiled in an enormous pot. This is how sailors made sure that each man got a fair share:

The Steward was responsible for dividing the crew into messes. Each gun crew would form a mess of between six and eight men. One person would collect the food for his mess in a large wooden bowl

Sailors used to eat from wooden bowls like these.

and the head of each mess would divide it into equal shares.

The rations would keep a man fit to fight during short battle campaigns. The food was probably better than he would have eaten on land. But the lack of fresh fruit and vegetables led to an illness called scurvy.

Doctor at sea

Inside a ship there was little fresh air, no fridge and no antibiotic medicine. Even if food and water went bad it still had to be eaten. Many sailors became ill – more people died at sea from disease than from injury.

From the middle of the sixteenth century large ships had a Barber-Surgeon among the crew. He kept a well-equipped medicine chest in order to treat all common illnesses and wounds on board the ship. He was also the ship's Barber!

The medicine chest found on the *Mary Rose* contained wooden ointment jars which still had ointment inside. There were also narrow-necked jugs sealed with corks. These may have contained medicine.

A medicine chest was found on the *Mary Rose*. It was in the Barber-Surgeon's cabin on the main gun deck close to action stations. If a man was wounded during a battle, it was easy to take him to the cabin for treatment.

(Left) Many of the seamen's chests on the *Mary Rose* contained peppercorns. Spices like pepper were used to flavour food and to help digestion.

On later ships like the *Wasa*, the Barber-Surgeon's cabin was below the water-line in a section of the hold called the orlop deck. It was further away from the battle than the Barber-Surgeon's cabin on the *Mary Rose*. But it did keep wounded men away from the men who were still busy fighting the enemy.

The main danger was from wounds becoming infected. If this happened the infected part was cut off. The person often died later from loss of blood or from another infection.

The basic equipment used by the Barber-Surgeon remained the same for centuries. New medicines and drugs were made, though, which gave the patient a better chance of staying alive.

(Below) If a sailor had a high temperature the Barber-Surgeon would take some of his blood from a vein. This was thought to stop the fever. He used a bleeding bowl like this one to catch the blood.

The tools they used

Carpenters were needed on a ship to keep it in good repair. They often had to stop leaks and repair wooden parts of the ship that were damaged. If a seam between two planks began to open up it could be caulked (sealed) with a sealing mixture of strands of rope and pitch.

Most leaks in large wooden ships were caused by running aground. If the keel touched the sea-bed a seam could burst open and leak. Carpenters would caulk the seam from the inside to hold the leak until the ship could be brought into shallow water. Then the ship would be laid over on her side to be recaulked from the outside and patched with a lead tingle (patch).

Sixteenth-century carpentry tools.

I Brace; part of a brace and bit used for drilling holes.

2 Rule

3 Whetstone, for sharpening tools.

4 Mallet

5 Planes for smoothing and shaping wood.

6 Nails

7 Tool for marking where to cut wood.

Often on a long voyage the Carpenter would have to build a small boat to replace one lost by accident. The small boat, or shallop, was needed to send men between one ship and another, to lay out a second anchor to help to secure the ship, and to take men ashore to explore unknown lands.

(Above) **A brass lodestone from the 1500s. It was used to keep the compass needle magnetic on a long voyage.**

It was the duty of the Pilot to bring a ship into harbour or to find a safe place to anchor. He used a simple tool called a lead line, or sound, to measure the depth of the water. He took a small sample of the sea-bed so that he could tell whether the bottom was sand, mud or rock. Lead lines have been used for at least 2,000 years.

This modern drawing shows the Pilot on a Tudor ship. He is using a lead line to measure the depth of the water.

Ropes, rigging and sails

Throughout the Tudor and Stuart period ships and boats could only be moved using sails or oars. Both methods involved muscle and manpower. Large ships usually had four masts with heavy sails supported from yards. Many men were needed to raise and lower the sails.

To raise and lower a sail a series of pulleys and lines were used. Seamen had to learn how to secure a line and tie a knot which was safe but could be released quickly. Working high above the deck of a ship that was pitching and tossing in the waves was dangerous – a badly-tied knot could cause a disaster.

Some of the most useful knots are still used today by sailors, mountaineers, fishermen and divers.

1. Make a loop in the rope.

2. Pass right-hand tail through the loop and behind the rope.

3. Pass tail over the bottom of the loop and pull tight.

A bowline is a secure loop. It is used today to tie a safety line for a crew member on a sailing boat or to make a safety line for a diver.

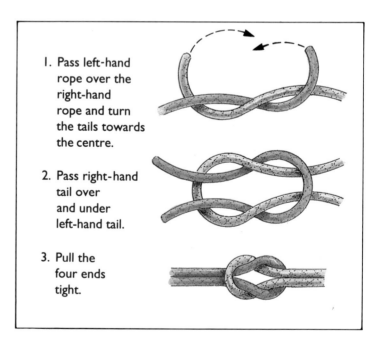

1. Pass left-hand rope over the right-hand rope and turn the tails towards the centre.

2. Pass right-hand tail over and under left-hand tail.

3. Pull the four ends tight.

The reef knot is used to join two ropes of equal thickness.

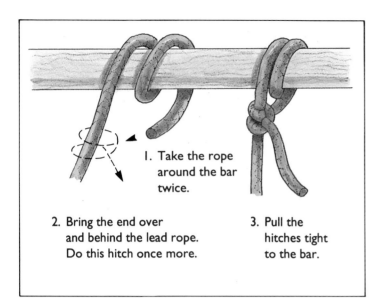

1. Take the rope around the bar twice.

2. Bring the end over and behind the lead rope. Do this hitch once more.

3. Pull the hitches tight to the bar.

(Above) A round turn and two half hitches is used to tie a rope to a bar or ring. It is useful when tying up the boat.

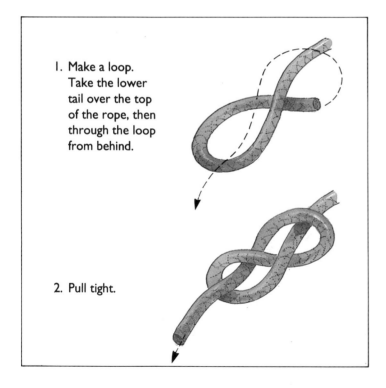

1. Make a loop. Take the lower tail over the top of the rope, then through the loop from behind.

2. Pull tight.

A figure of eight is a stop knot used to prevent a rope passing through an opening.

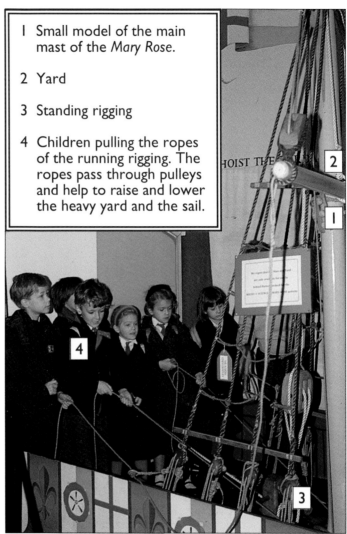

1 Small model of the main mast of the *Mary Rose*.

2 Yard

3 Standing rigging

4 Children pulling the ropes of the running rigging. The ropes pass through pulleys and help to raise and lower the heavy yard and the sail.

(Above) Children using pulleys on a scale model of a Tudor mast and yard.

Above is a model of a Tudor mast and yard. The standing rigging holds and supports the mast. The running rigging is used to raise and lower the yards which carry the sails. By using a series of pulleys the load can be reduced and raising the sails becomes easier.

Clues from shipwrecks

Direct evidence for life at sea in the past can be recovered from shipwrecks. If a wreck is carefully excavated much more 'treasure' can be found than just a few gold coins and some guns. A modern archaeologist tries to recover all the evidence.

Many human bones have been recovered from shipwrecks. From bones we can estimate how old and tall a man was. We can answer other questions too:

Was he strong? Did he have powerful muscles? Marks where the muscles were attached can be seen on the long bones of the arms and legs. Did he have a healthy diet when he was young? If the bones and teeth are badly formed, we know the person had a poor diet.

A model of the *Boyne*, as it looked in 1692. This kind of decoration is often found on ships from that time.

Sometimes, as in the *Mary Rose*, skeletons are found with clothing. Leather shoes and leather jerkins (jackets) survive well if they have been buried in a muddy sea-bed. From these we can judge if a man was an officer or a seaman. Some men trapped on the gun decks were found with swords and knives. Traces of iron stain in the mud suggest that they wore armour.

We can learn about life on board a ship from the remains of food stored in casks and from cooking utensils.

A face carved on a wooden panel, found in 1992 in the wreck of a warship. The warship had sunk close to the Isle of Mull, Scotland, in 1652.

There might also be leather book-covers, musical instruments or the skeleton of a small dog. Even the dried grass, stuffed in a sack to make a bed, gives us evidence of the grasses and flowers which once grew in a hayfield.

Sealed in a shipwreck is rubbish, such as leaves, seeds and dead insects, as well as treasure. The rubbish probably tells us more about life on the ship that sank than the treasure ever will.

Clues from models and writings

There are no plans or drawings from the beginning of the Tudor period to show us how ships were built then. We have to study early ship models and paintings to see how the shape of ships changed and how the sails altered.

Letters written on board ship often tell of shortages of food and equipment because the supply boats had not arrived. We can read poetry, which gives us an idea of how people thought about ships and sea battles.

A drawing by Matthew Baker from the late sixteenth century. It shows that a ship is the same kind of shape as a fish. It is one of the earliest English shipbuilders' drawings to show the shape of ships.

One long poem (called *The Ballad of Sir Andrew Barton*) describes a sea fight between Sir Edward Howard, an English Sea Captain, and Andrew Barton, a Scottish Captain, in 1511. The merchants of London complained that Andrew Barton would not let their merchant ships cross the English Channel to France. He was capturing their ships and seizing goods, which was bad for trade!

The poem describes how, at King Henry VIII's command, Sir Howard chose his crew. He included gunners, archers and soldiers armed with pikes.

A model of the *Mary Rose* as she was in 1545. There is no decoration on the ship.

The sea battle was hard. Drums, whistles and trumpets were played to encourage the men. Towards the end Andrew Barton was killed by an English archer and his ship was seized as a prize. The King made Horslay, the archer, a knight and gave him lands. Success in war often brought riches to the winner.

A model of the *Prince*, a ship which was built in 1670. This ship was beautifully decorated at the stern (at the right of the picture).

Finding out more

Many museums and art galleries have models and paintings of ships which help us to understand how people lived and worked on them. Some contain objects that have been preserved, including material and equipment from shipwrecks. The evidence builds together just like in a detective story.

Paintings like this one by Adam Willaerts (1577–1669) tell us a lot about ships and the people who worked on them. Here, seamen and officers are saying goodbye to their families before going back to their ship, *HMS Prince Royal*.

(Below) A painting of ships at sea by Adam Willaerts, 1640.

Map labels: Edinburgh, Liverpool, King's Lynn, Felixstowe, London, Deal, Dover, Hastings, Southampton, Portsmouth, Bridport, Teignmouth, Poole, Falmouth

(Above) This map shows where you can go in Britain to find out about the navies of Tudor and Stuart times.

26

This is Deal Castle, which was built by Henry VIII at Walmer in Kent. It was one of a chain of fortifications he had built to guard the English coastline and to stop a French invasion.

Deal Castle, which was built in 1540.

This is one of a chain of beacons lit in England in 1988 to celebrate the 400th anniversary of the defeat of the Spanish Armada. Beacons had been lit in 1588 to warn people that the Spanish were invading.

You can still see beacons along the south coast of England.

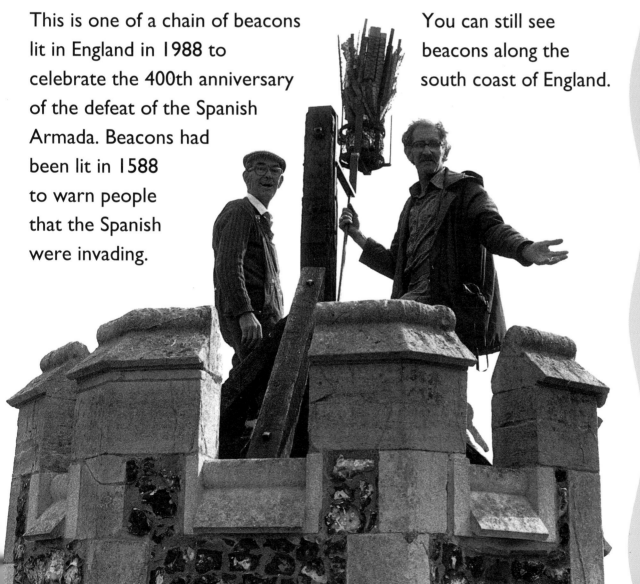

Timeline

1588
The Spanish Armada is defeated by the English fleet

1590
The *Hopewell* sets sail for America.

1660
The English fighting fleets are now called the Royal Navy.

1670
The *Prince* is built.

Timeline

| 1480 | 1500 | 1520 | 1540 | 1560 | 1580 |

Tudors

1485 HENRY VII

1509 HENRY VIII

1547 EDWARD VI
1553 MARY TUDOR
1558 ELIZABETH I

1480–1500	1500–1520	1520–1540	1540–1560	1560–1580	1580–1600
1487 John Cabot's first voyage from Bristol to Newfoundland (now part of Canada).	**1509** Cabot tries to sail round the North of Canada.	**1520** Spanish people begin to settle on the American mainland.	**1544** The siege of Boulogne, France, by the English Army.	**1576** Martin Frobisher's first voyage in search of the north-west passage round the north of Canada.	**1584** An English settlement is established by Sir Walter Raleigh at Roanoke in North Carolina.
1492 The first globe is made in Nuremberg, Germany by Martin Behaim.	**1509** Work begins on building the *Mary Rose* in Portsmouth.	**1534** Henry VIII becomes Head of the Church in England and Wales.	**1545** The *Mary Rose* sinks while going into action against a French invasion fleet.	**1577** Sir Francis Drake sets off on his voyage around the world.	**1588** The Spanish Armada is defeated by the English.
1492 Christopher Columbus sails to America.	**1517** Portuguese sailors reach China by a sea route.	**1536–39** Henry VIII has the monasteries destroyed.	**1546** The Navy Board is founded to maintain the English fleet.		**1590** John White sails in the *Hopewell* to North Carolina to aid any survivors from the settlement at Roanoke.
1495 The first dry dock is built at Portsmouth. (A dry dock is a dock cut off from the sea where ships can be mended or built.)			**1547–53** Many schools and colleges are built.		**1590–1616** William Shakespeare writes his plays.
			1554 Battista Agnese makes the first chart of the world showing latitude and longitude.		

1600 1620 1640 1660 1680 1700

Stuarts

1603 JAMES I
(JAMES VI OF
SCOTLAND)

1625 CHARLES I

1649–1660 COMMONWEALTH
1653 OLIVER CROMWELL

1658 RICHARD CROMWELL

1660 CHARLES II

1685 JAMES II

1688 WILLIAM III & MARY II

1702–1714 ANNE

1600–1620	1620–1640	1640–1660	1660–1680	1680–1700	1700–1720
1605 The Gunpowder Plot. **1610** Henry Hudson discovers a huge bay in Northern Canada. It is named Hudson Bay after him.	**1620** The Puritan Pilgrim Fathers sail from Plymouth to settle in America. **1629–40** King Charles I rules without Parliament. **1634** Charles I orders the *Sovereign of the Seas* to be built at Woolwich. She is larger and better armed than all earlier ships.	**1642** The English Civil War begins. **1646** Charles I is captured. He is imprisoned at Carisbrooke Castle the following year. **1649** Charles I is imprisoned at Hurst Castle before being taken to London for trial and execution.	**1660** Charles II becomes king. **1660** The English fighting fleets are now called the Royal Navy. **1665** The plague. **1666** The Great Fire of London. **1667–95** The composer Henry Purcell writes his music.	**1688** William III and Mary II are crowned. James II flees England. **1690** James II is defeated by William III at the Battle of the Boyne in Ireland.	**1707** England and Scotland are officially united.

Glossary

Action stations The positions soldiers and sailors go to for fighting battles.

Advantage of the wind To have the wind behind the sails in order to make good speed.

Archer A person who fights with bow and arrows.

Bosun (Boatswain) The officer who keeps the ship and its equipment in good repair.

Bow The front of a ship.

Caulk To seal the seams between planks using hair or oakum (rope strands) and pitch.

Excavate To dig up buried evidence to find out about the past.

Fortification A place built to be strong. Soldiers were based there to defend the area against attack.

Hold The bottom of a ship, below the decks, where goods can be stored.

Keel Long piece of wood that stretches along the bottom of a ship, holding it together.

Master The officer who is responsible for steering the ship and navigating.

Merchant ship A ship used for carrying passengers and goods.

Mess A group of people who eat together.

Musketeer A soldier armed with a light handgun called a musket.

Navigation Method of finding the position and course of a ship or aircraft.

Orlop deck The lowest deck of the ship, which is below the water-line. Used for storing spare weapons and food.

Pitch A substance like tar.

Quartermaster The officer in charge of supplies and storing them properly in the hold.

Stern The back of a ship.

Water-line Line on a ship where the water reaches when the ship is in water.

Yard A wooden beam which crosses the mast and supports the sail.

Places to visit

Museums

Bridgewater, Somerset Admiral Blake Museum; tel. 0278 456127. Oliver Cromwell's home during the Commonwealth period. Contains many of his personal possessions, including a compass and papers.

Bridport, Dorset Centre for rope and net making; tel. 0308 22116. A museum in a Tudor house.

Edinburgh The National Museum of Scotland, Chambers Street; tel. 031 225 7534.

Falmouth, Cornwall Pendennis Castle; tel. 0326 316594. Fort built by Henry VIII to defend the harbour. Guns and gunnery equipment similar to those found on the *Mary Rose.*

Hastings, E. Sussex Shipwreck Heritage Centre, Rock-A-Nore Road, TN34 3DW; tel. 0424 437452.

Liverpool Merseyside Maritime Museum, Albert Dock; tel. 051 207 0001. Demonstrations of crafts including sail and rope-making, and barrel-making.

London
Museum of London, London Wall, London EC2Y 5HN; tel. 071 600 3699.

The National Maritime Museum, Greenwich, SE10 0NF; tel. 081 858 4422. Ship models and paintings. Town seals with pictures of ships. Navigation equipment.

Science Museum, South Kensington, London SW72DD; tel. 071 938 8000. Models of ships and docks. Navigation and diving equipment. Early medical chests.

Poole, Dorset Waterfront Museum, Paradise Street; tel. 0202 683 138. Shipwreck material and timbers recovered from a sixteenth-century armed merchant ship in Poole Bay.

Portsmouth The Mary Rose Museum, Royal Naval Base, Portsmouth; tel. 0705 751520. The remains of a mid sixteenth-century warship and the weapons, clothing and personal possessions of the soldiers and seamen who drowned when she sank.

Southampton The Tudor Merchant's House, Bugle St, Southampton; tel. 0703 224216.

Teignmouth, Devon Teignmouth District Canal Museum. Material from a late sixteenth-century wreck which is being excavated in the bay. Open summer months only.

Yelverton, Devon Buckland Abbey, Yelverton PL20 6EY; tel. 0822 853607. House owned by Sir Richard Grenville in 1576 and by Sir Francis Drake in 1581. The museum contains ship models and Drake's drum.

Fort
Felixstowe, Suffolk Sixteenth-century fort on Landguard Point.
Sites
King's Lynn, Norfolk Customs House (1683) and merchants' houses.
Southwold, Suffolk Overlooks site of the Battle of Sole Bay (1672). Guns were sent by King Charles I to defend the town against French armed ships.

Books to read

Adams, S. *Exploration and Empire* (Kingfisher, 1990)

Blandford, P. *New Explorer's Guide to Maps and Compasses* (TAB Books, USA, 1992)

Coote, R. *Tudor Sailors* (Wayland, 1989)

Morrison, I. *Mary Rose: Her Wreck and Rescue* (Lutterworth, 1988)

Ships and Sailing (Dorling Kindersley, 1991)

Triggs, T.D. *Tudor Britain* (Wayland, 1989)

Tudor Seafarers (Oxford University Press, 1989)

Index

Words in **bold** are subjects shown in pictures as well as in the text.